ADVENT~~CHRISTMAS

A Pilgrimage of Light

ADVENT ~~ CHRISTMAS

A Pilgrimage of Light

Sister Ave Clark, O.P.

Sister Ave Clark, O.P.
Heart to Heart Ministry
718-428-2471
Pearlbud7@aol.com
www.h2h.nyc

Rachel Prayer Hour: post-abortion syndrome
Elizabeth Ministry: for parents who lost a child
Caring Hearts: for people with PTSD
ROSES: for survivors of abuse/domestic violence
ACOA: for adult children of alcoholics
Caritas: for family with children/adult with a
        disability
Lights in the Darkness: for persons seeking healing
        from depression
Bereavement Sessions: From the Heart (individual)
Spiritual Direction: Open Your Heart (individual)
Pastoral Prayer-line: A Listening Heart
Podcast Nun: Everyday Graces
Podcast Nun 2: Heart Conversations
Heart to Heart Prayer Chats: Across the Country

Only the wings of love and compassion
can lift and carry us.

The Advent~~Christmas Lights

Calls us forth...
> ...to leave the comfortable
> ...to let go of self-centeredness
> ...to a creative holy space of
> "newness"

This wonderful Pilgrimage of Light
> encourages transformative change~~
not to be great...but to be more gracious
not to be powerful...but to empower one
> another to be better
not to be first...but to join the least and
> receive a new perspective on life

IN MEMORY

Sister Lucille D'Amelio, O.P, my very dear
Dominican sister-friend for many decades.
Lucille enjoyed the lights that led her to serve
God in a variety of ways. I know that her light
of faith led her to her heavenly home.

"I thank my God whenever I think of you"
(Philippians 1-3)

TABLE OF CONTENTS

Special Message: Advent is a special season. Its' lights lead us to the wonderful and holy place of Christ being born in our human heart. As you hold each light of this Advent~~Christmas season let your journey become brighter each day.

Personal Reflections: are sprinkled throughout this book with some pilgrim friends sharing their journey of faith. You might even write a few thoughts about your pilgrimage with a light.

Chapters: the chapters in this book will not be given a page number in the content. The author invites you to open to a special titled page or any other page and reflect on the meaning of these wondrous Advent lights in your life.

DEDICATION

☆☆ **Sister Martin Marie Doran, O.P**
Her <u>light of love</u> gently touches our world with a sense of great caring. Wherever Sister Martin is … she lights up the room with her holy presence of sharing Jesus' love.

☆☆ **Frank Orlando**
Despite any difficulties or trials Frank always has hope.   Perhaps it is Frank's inner faith that stirs the <u>light of hope</u> so that others can be hope-filled too.

☆☆ **Sister Selenia Quinones, O.P.**
Sister Selenia has a beautiful quality of joy. I truly believe that it is born in her prayer life. This <u>light of joy</u> is spread by her graciousness of spirit.

☆☆ **Nelson Villatoro**
Nelson is a man who knows that the <u>light of peace</u> brings blessings. His peace is especially exhibited in his deep caring for his special-needs daughter, Swammy. Nelson trusts in God's peace.

PROLOGUE

Being a wise Mother, the Church sets aside four weeks before Christmas for us "to prepare the way of the Lord". How thoughtful ~~ how caring! This year, let's journey together with the Holy Family ~~ Jesus, Mary and Joseph and prepare our hearts especially for the coming of our Savior.

One way to begin is by using candles, one for each week, three white (or purple) and one pink. The pink candle is for the third week to remind us that the time is nearly here ~~ are we ready? Another way is the use of a calendar with a thought or word to keep us focused. Another way is to find a good book that will help us remember what Advent is really about...preparation.

Let's try to get close to some (or all) Christmas people. In our prayers and readings we will meet lots of people who will help us to get our hearts in order ~~ Jesus, Mary, Joseph, Angels, Shepherds, kings even animals, all have a part and all will bring us closer to Jesus on his birthday. Just think if we could stay really close to Mary for just one day; how she would help us to prepare well. Think what an important part the sheep, the oxen, and the shepherds were for this important event.

The thing is, we have only these four weeks we have to be ready. We have to make sure that each day we start off aware of the journey, aware what will keep us on the right road just for that day. In the end we will be thrilled that we took the time and the effort to prepare as we greet the Lord on His day...Christmas day. Come, Lord Jesus!

Sister Martin Marie Doran, O.P.

" ...for unto you is born this day in the City of David a Savior, who is Christ the Lord~~ You will find a baby wrapped in

swaddling clothes and lying in a manger..."
(Luke 2:8-14)

Each day of Advent let us...

...carry a light

...tend to a light

...proclaim a light

...shelter a light

...search for a light

...share a light

...receive a light

...find a light

...pray with a light

...become a light

The Advent Wreath began as a German custom going back to the 1800's   Brought to the United States in the 20's or 30's, a pine wreath decorated with cones and berries and 4 candles (3 purple, 1 pink). The first candle was lit on the First Sunday of Advent and the others lit on the following three Sundays.

When my children were very young, the Advent Wreath was a good way of turning their attention away from thinking too early of toys and stockings hung by the fireplace. Instead, the wreath helped us to focus on Advent and prepare for Jesus coming on Christmas day. We'd meet at the dining room table, light the first purple candle on the first Sunday and each Sunday after, light another. The pink candle was lit on the third Sunday because it meant that we were halfway to Christmas (Gaudete Sunday). We'd talk about the thousands of years the world had been waiting for Jesus, about Mary saying yes to the angel, how happy we are that Jesus is coming, and the peace that he would be bringing. This little ceremony was not long. The children were usually antsy, but it was a good way of slowing down and reminding them of what was truly important.

Mary Anne Dougherty

If you close your eyes, you can imagine yourself at that table and deepen your awareness of what truly is important in life...sharing your faith. What better way to take this holy...

Advent~~Christmas Pilgrimage of Light

Author's Note

ADVENT LIGHTS ~~ They direct us.

They show us a path that is...
       ...holy
       ...faith-filled
       ...hopeful
       ...prophetic

Advent Lights lead us on a journey of renewal. They call us forth into a world in need of lights that heal and soothe, encourage and bless all who yearn and long for the peace of the Creator's love.

Advent Lights <u>invite</u> us to be Jesus' love here on earth.
Advent Lights <u>mission</u> us to bear the message of peace to all humankind.
Advent Lights <u>empower</u> us to reveal the presence of hope born in our daily life.
Advent Lights <u>gift</u> us with the necessary graces to carry the lights out into the world.

I asked different pilgrim friends to share their thoughts on Advent and Christmas time so that the readers of this book (and myself) could reflect more deeply on how everyone is called to be part of the Pilgrimage of Light by becoming part of the celebration of Jesus being reborn again and again in every human heart.

Advent is a wonderful, holy and life-giving season that shows each one of us that waiting and preparing our hearts can be the best part of the pilgrimage of Christmas time.

Advent is a heart-to-heart pilgrimage

Advent is a time of stillness, waiting and watching. During this holy season prepare your heart to welcome the Lord who comes to us every day in the stillness of a quiet dawn and deep winter sunset.

When we welcome the Lord ~~
He comes into the manger of an open,
        gentle, believing heart.
Let us be aware of the "now" moment of our pilgrim journey.

Now …. is the moment to look at each day and week of this Advent time and to become a bright, holy reflection of the marvelous Light that came to bring peace on earth.

Be Still
   and know that God
   is always with you

What do you hear in the stillness?

What light is your favorite and why?

How do you share the light in your daily life?

Write a prayer called Advent Stillness.

The Advent Wreath

The leaves are all gone
The trees are barren and bare
The autumn winds are chilling
Yet anticipation's everywhere
It is the Advent season
The winter nights grow near
We search for the warmth inside ourselves
Wreaths are everywhere
Cousins to our Christmas trees
That bring us joy and brilliance
We place them in and on our homes
And they remind us of resilience
Circular in shape
Symbols of connection
That despite the cold and dark of night
We'll find light and resurrection.

(James Palmaro, a gifted poet with words formed by the light of love written in prose. He himself is disabled with blindness and sees the world through his faith-lived well.)

Advent~~Christmas

Christ came and took on a human face …
What a gift of grace to see Christ in one another. God lives in our humanity and so our challenge is to bring Jesus' love to life in our human hearts and become more aware that we each are the face of God reborn.

Jesus is born and reborn in our heart especially during the Advent season forever giving us the promise of God's Gift of unconditional love. New life, new hope, wonderful joy, and new paths of peace to take by rediscovering holy ways of living our faithfulness. Like Jesus, let us continue to take the holy pilgrimage to the heart of Bethlehem and become a dazzling light of Jesus love here on earth.

What does "dazzling" mean to you?

A dazzling thought...

Advent is a holy time for me. The lighting of the Advent candles each Sunday before Christmas gives me a time of reflection of the past and hope for the future. I find that Advent time is a time of preparation of my heart, mind and soul for Christ's arrival in a world as it is today. As I am getting older and more mature in my faith, I pray and sacrifice and share by listening more deeply to the message of the gospels.

These Advent lights come together combining the dazzling hope and love, peace and joy of Jesus being reborn in our hearts. Let your heart choose during this holy season to be inspired to decorate the world with kindness and compassion for all.

Joseph Clark

Yes, this is my younger brother...he sure dazzles the world with his joyous spirit and not just during the Advent ~~ Christmas time ... but every day.

St. Elizabeth ~~

    "blessed are you among women..."

                (Luke 1:42)

Elizabeth embraced Mary at a time when both women felt vulnerable. Together they were strengthened by their faithfulness. They rejoiced in the "impossibility" that each one of them was experiencing and to give birth to God's love.

Think of what has seemed "impossible" or difficult in your life. How does your faith help to give you the light of "possibility"?

Just as one candle lights another and can
light 1000 of other candles
so, one heart can illuminate another and
can illuminate 1000 more hearts.

...a mother helping her disabled daughter
get into a car by lifting her
...a homeless man sharing a place on
a park bench

The light is so brilliant.
So is God's love 1000 X 1000.
And in your very soul of being
are sparks of the Divine light
These endless sparks can spread joy
and hope, peace and love throughout
the Universe.

How do you carry your light?
1.
2.

Where is your light needed?
1.
2.

The Advent ~~ Christmas light is...
...welcoming
...soft, tender and gentle

It has a common center of...
...tranquility and harmony
...unity of spirit

The light shines...
...peace and justice
...mercy and compassion

This light is bright with faith shared...
...through our humble deeds and words
...gracious gestures and courageous acts of
        charity

This light that shines so deeply...
...does not fade
...rekindles hope again and again and again

Name a time in your life that this light
beckoned you, called you forth, and invited
you to shine in ways that would bring peace
and celebrate peace.

The light shines in any darkness of...
...discouragement
...fear
...loss
...hardship
...transition

Our faith helps us to hold and carry this light. God's Divine light holds and carries us. Advent comes during the darkest time of the year as the days get shorter approaching Christmas. It's a difficult time of year for me, as I always feel sad by the lack of sunlight and stressed by the preparations for Christmas. That is the secular part of the season. Fortunately, there is a spiritual side to it. This is the part that really counts.

Advent is the time when we "await in joyful hope for the coming of our Savior, Jesus Christ." For me, Advent means waiting patiently while preparing myself spiritually for the Son/Sun to come and brighten our world.

Paula Santoro

How will you bring the Son/Sun light into your life and the lives of others during this Advent ~~ Christmas season?

List 3 practical ways.
1.
2.
3.

John the Baptist...

> tells us to make the path straight.

What is the name of this path in your life?

What voices do we hear today that resonate

> with the voice of John the Baptist?

Are they voices that speak for...

> ...justice and mercy

>> ...honesty and integrity

>>> ...compassion and charity

Just think...we are all called.

> When our small light can dare to make a positive impact on those around the world seeking justice, creating peace, we too can become immersed in sharing the Bethlehem light of love.

How do you give voice to the light of love
right where you are?

It is this year's Advent more than ever, that we can more closely relate to the joyous waiting as we wait for yet another big blessing to our family … the birth of a fourth grandchild, the long awaited and prayed for sibling to our youngest grandchild, 10-year-old Miguel, who is currently the only child of our youngest son and his wife. This wonderful news of new birth to come has inspired us during this Advent season to pray that it is an intentional life-transforming time. We pray to be witnesses of love, mercy and faithfulness and to be life-bearers of the Good News to those around us. We are living in a world of much chaos, uncertainties, difficulties and divisions. We pray with the first light of Advent called HOPE that we can be bearers of hope in this world of darkness as we share the goodness of God. We truly believe that Jesus' persistent love is the forever source of hope reborn time and time again and brings deep joy.

Tessie and Rudy Sugaste

Hope

What Good News can you share in joyous ways that encourage others to feel the presence of the holy light of Hope?

Coming, anticipation, excitement....
not so much these as ~~ waiting.

Waiting~~Advent is more about waiting. Waiting is an active stance. Doing, maybe doing internally, inside. Thinking back to growing up we always put up a manger. That's probably one of the most meaningful symbols for me and my favorite Advent light~~the light in the stable.

I read an Advent reflection once titled: "Shipwrecked at the Stable". I know the title sounds kind of weird. The idea is we come to the stable to receive. The stable has the whole Holy Family there. We have a special devotion to the Holy Family. And it's actually the first time the Holy Family is altogether. We just give all our needs and difficulties. We receive strength for our life pilgrimage.

Advent means come as you are but do come! For us, Advent includes Michael (our son who died at 21 of suicide). Two of our other sons Phil and Paul's birthdays and the anniversary of Michael's death just two days before Christmas. If that weren't too much, it was also in the first week of Advent at age 11 that my (and Dan's) father died. It left a deep impression on us. Early December, Advent has almost always been dark and difficult time, But, at the same time a hopeful time.

Longing, longing for loved ones no longer with us. The song, "There is a Longing in My Heart" is a great song about all this. Here are some of the words:

There's a longing in my heart, Lord.
There's a thirsting in my soul.
As the deer longs for the water,
Thou O Lord, I long to know.

The other song that speaks about just coming to the stable is: "Come As You Are"

Lay down your burdens. Lay down your
shame.
All who are broken, lift up your face.
Oh wanderer, come home. You're not too
far.
Lay down your hurt, lay down your heart.
Come as you are.

My mother was a great example of faith lived-well. Looking sad as we sat in a beautifully lit church on Christmas Eve, I asked her what was wrong. I think she conveyed all the loss, all the missing, all the longing in a few words. "When you're older, you'll understand." Now I do.

Advent is waiting and longing, sorrow and hope. Perhaps it's best summed up in a repeating line from the song "Come as You Are" …

Earth has no sorrow that heaven can't heal. So, as you come to the stable and kneel with your hurting heart and loss…know that the peace of the Holy Family and our family are right there with you.

(Dan and Patty Callahan)

Remember the light becomes more brilliant as we give birth to love…even in darkness.

Search for shelter in the Advent~~Christmas lights and there you will discover that even darkness is radiant with the Holy light.

Darkness comes into life...
   We must...
      ...be vigilant
      ...protect the light
      ...cherish the light
      ...nurture the light

It is in usually in simple ways that we
   become more of the light with...
      ...charity and clarity
      ...reverence for all of life
      ...thoughtfulness
      ...goodness shared

Divine light streams down
and out~~
...down from the Heavens
...out into the world

This is the light that you and I are given freely. Let your light stream out into the world the message of Bethlehem's love every day.

Name some ordinary ways in which you can stream out
    the love of the Lord in...
       ...forgiving ways
       ...healing ways
       ...peaceful ways

A Holy Time...

It is a time to find peace and love for all and to enjoy life. This holy time of Advent~~ Christmas season invites each one of us to actively share the unconditional love the Lord has given us so generously. The best way I think I could share Christ's love is by being there in caring ways for others and listening with an open heart.

Another aspect of this holy time is to share forgiveness and receive it in life-giving and respectful ways. The third light of the Advent wreath is my favorite. It just stands out the most (pink in color) and deepens my joy that is born of God's unconditional love.

I pray that I can be a messenger with the light of peace and joy not just during this holy season but every day of the year.

Come, Lord Jesus, into my
♥ today.

Daniel Goiz
Bayside Farm Deli
...server of Joy

An Advent Prayer-filled Message...

The Advent~~Christmas season is all about reflecting on how we can prepare our hearts and homes. It is a wondrous time for each one of us to deepen our awareness of the true meaning of Jesus' birth.

Let us take time each day of Advent to pray for the guidance to be compassionate and to evangelize by our ordinary deeds of *kindness.* This holy season reminds us to look beyond ourselves, expanding our mind and hearts in order to open ourselves up to the needs of others.

Lord Jesus master of both the light and the darkness...send your spiritual lights upon our humble and very human Christmas preparations so that we might seek some quiet space to hear your voice...telling us that Jesus is born right where you are. Amen.

Frank Orlando

♡

I believe that the Advent~~Christmas season is a holy time of wonderful renewal to till the soil of our spiritual lives…holy reading, meditating, praying a few beads on the rosary, doing a novena, sharing a quiet visit at church and quiet holy time at home to light your Advent wreath with a holy action of peace shared each day.

What is your peace-action today?

Name some ordinary deeds you can share during this Advent~~Christmas season right where you are.

Advent Lights remind us to trust in hope, love, joy and peace. Let these lights dwell deeply in your heart-spirit. Let's think of those people who need comfort, consolation, healing and affirmation. A call, an email, a card or a whispered prayer are wonderful, caring gifts to give, share and receive.

Just imagine the shining of the light as...
...a blessing of joy
...a grace of love
...a gift of hope
...a whisper of charity
...a touch of compassion
...a gaze of deep understanding
...a prayer of forgiveness
...a nod of kind respect
...a reflection of mercy

> Just imagine all the ways you can
> encounter the light of Jesus' love.

How will you magnify the Lord today?
1.
2.
3.

The Warmth of the Light...

 The candle flame of Advent gives off warmth as well as light and that warmth symbolizes the closeness of Jesus. God's son is God beyond comprehension, but he comes to us as an infant, not in His immenseness, so that we can hold him in closeness and experience the warmth of His presence. He comes as one of us in the gift of birth so that He may share His life, His love, indeed His divinity, just as He shares our humanity.

Such closeness, such warmth, such a gift! The appropriate response from us should be Thank You! Thank You for being close to me in the reality of faith-shared. Thank You for your redemptive gift. My pledge is to tell others by what I say and what I do with the warmth of this precious love...that your gift, Lord, is full of the warmth of redeeming and restorative love. Amen.

Joseph (Joe) Dougherty

How would you describe the "warmth" of Jesus love?

How do you share this "warmth"?

The Radiance of the Message

We say…Come, Lord Jesus
You are welcome here
We await your coming
Come Lord, Jesus
and on that day a branch shall
     spring like a loving kind word
a sign of hope that brings new life
     with unity and harmony for all
and those who seek, yearn
     and hope shall rise
with a new dawn
a light will shine
for those who walk among
the gloom of despair
and in any way we be lame of heart
     or deaf or blind
to the wonderful message of
     God with us
God keeps calling

Come   Come   Come Follow Me
and when we do…the radiance
is truly the Love of God

Be the Radiance of the Message

My God, My Savior

The Magnificat is the Prayer of Mary. Mary's
prayer reveals the beauty and faith of her
soul and her humility of being chosen
     by God.
The Glory belongs to God.
We gather together to share
     the glory of the Radiant One
Let us, like Mary
 say: Yes   Yes   Yes
God's will ~~ God's way ~~ God's grace
Like Mary, the journey to Bethlehem where
Jesus is born is our journey. We discover
Bethlehem where life is born, renewed, and
graced. It is where God calls you (and me
too) to be His light...to say: Yes Yes Yes
The light restores, renews and re-energizes...
     ...our weakness becomes a strength
     ...our limitations become a gift
     ...our fears become a blessing of
       understanding.

*All wrapped in the humble and ordinary
light of our humanity illuminated by our
faith-lived well.*

Mary and the Advent Pilgrimage

Like Mary, let your Advent begin with a Yes to God. Let us together hold the sacred lights of this holy season and once again give birth to a magnifying light of trusting in God's ways…in our daily lives.

Our Yes can be radiant and joyous; it can also struggle and fumble a bit, but it is there being steadfast as a sign of…

    …encouragement
    …comfort
    …support
    …compassion

Mary shows us how to embrace a divine call to be Jesus' Yes in today's world. Take your light out into the world as Mary did… "according to the Word". Mary shows us that when you open your heart you will discover…

    …a wonderful capacity to care deeply
    …a way to be generous with your time,
        presence and love
    …a way to engage the difficulties of
        everyday life with deep patience
        grounded in mercy and compassion

Yes   Yes   Yes

Mary gave us many holy examples of saying Yes with a trusting heart. Sometimes our Yes is said not knowing everything but believing it is for the best.

Here are two questions to help us say Yes.
1. Is it good for you/for others?
2. Is it life-giving?

A Yes from a loving, faithful heart...
        ...provides hope
        ...gives comfort
        ...sets healthy boundaries
        ...is generous of spirit
        ...is full of God- graciousness

When you pray and ponder (as Mary did)
        Your Yes will have...
                ...clarity
                ...purpose
                ...love in it
                ...faith in it

These are not just thoughts for Advent; these are words that remind us of the daily call to be faithful disciples that hold the lights filled with...

> ...tenderness
> ...graciousness
> ...patient kindness
> ...courageous acts of giving mercy

Mary said, "my soul magnifies the Lord..." Let us become spiritual magnifiers...

> ...full of grace
> ...trusting in the unknown
> ...responding with hope
> ...daring to risk for the common good

The way of living as Mary did will empower us to...

> ...diminish any darkness in life
> ...enlighten divine love to be our center
> ...serve with charity and dignity
> ...give joy away by affirming goodness in others
> ...forgive from your heart-peace
> ...be encouraging not judgmental

Aaaah Faith ~~ a strong, brilliant and valiant light. This is the light that Mary shone ever so brightly as she now shows us how to bring heavenly love to earth.

Here are people who share Mary-Presence
Celeste Grillo
Sister Audrey Harsen, O.P.
Nina Siggia
Monica Callendar
Mrs. T. Vitalis
Arlene Moss
Sister Carolann Masone, O.P.
Octavia Willis
Sister Marie Rabuse, O.P

Maryann Vilanti
Amy Lax
Sister Maureen Chase, O.P.
Mary Cesare
Sister Peggy Krajci, O.P.
Louise Mendenhall
Sister Lucille DeRosa, O.P.

Add your name to this list.

A Humble Presence

Jesus came as a baby needing 24/7 care
  A lesson of surrendering, trusting and accepting
  A lesson of loving, caring and holding the light of "presence"
God has done great things for us...

...coming to earth as a baby
...taking on human nature
...living simply and humbly
...reflecting goodness in all of humanity

Jesus came and walked among us as a friend, companion, pilgrim sojourner. During the Advent~~Christmas season we are told more about his presence of bestowing wonderful lights for all of us to hold, become and share. Just like the humble shepherds waking from sleep. Let us also be awake and more alert during this holy season and a bit more vigilant to hear the call and understand the manger scene as a holy presence of the stillness of life where we can find more of life.

Come, Let us adore

Don't you wish you could have been one of the shepherds on that first Christmas night... your heart full of wonder as you kneel and pray at the Nativity scene? Imagine yourself in that stable...

> It is quiet and still
> It is peaceful
> It is rich in joy and wonder
> It is truly a loving and hope-filled
> > place to be

Wherever and whenever you spread the joy of living and sharing the Gospel, that is a wonderful place to be... it is the sacred space of Bethlehem's lights.

As you light the Advent wreath... its' lights fill the night time of life.

The Shepherds and Advent

 The infancy narratives in Matthew (Magi) and Luke (shepherds), long conflated in our collective memory, lead us to presume that the shepherds saw the star that the Magi were following. No star in Luke! But there are angels ~~ and they sing.

Those angels announce the Good News to those shepherds and those shepherds make their way to Bethlehem to see what all the heavenly fuss is about. And after two millennia of Christian faith, the pious sight of humble shepherds kneeling before the Christ-child is seared into our minds. But what ever happened to those shepherds?

They see a new-born and then what? Back to those sheep ~~ there's work to do! There are no words, no teachings, no miraculous cures, no commandments, no religion connected with their encounter with this mystery shrouded in the ordinary. It's only the voices of the angels that make this most human of all events~~birth, pregnant with the possibility of an encounter with the transcendent. Or, perhaps, the angelic intervention suggests that, for most of us, the transcendent is only really found in ordinary human experience.

Given life expectancy in those days, very few if any of the shepherds would have still been alive when that baby grew into manhood and start his public ministry thirty years later.

Which means, of course, that the shepherds (as well as their counterparts, the Magi) encountered the divine without the aid of Christian religion, without doctrine or the dictates of morality. In this they bear affinity to our contemporaries who label themselves NONES, mainly young people who forego organized religion but still yearn for something they can't quite put their finger on ~~ an experience of the transcendent, a close encounter with a mystery that seems long abandoned by the rules and regulations of organized religion. In those shepherds they find fellow pilgrims.

 *"Religion can sometimes be the very thing that protects from the experience of God,"* **C.G. Jung once noted after spending countless hours in analysis with**

his religiously inclined patients. In this, Jung might have been echoing the insight Rudolf Otto formulated when he defined the HOLY as a mystery both fascinating and frightening. We know those shepherds were frightened because the angels had to command them: "Fear not." What captivates them however is nothing particularly extraordinary. And therein lies the great revelation of Advent. Divinity and humanity fit together so much like hand-in-glove that we often do not see it; the kingdom of heaven, as the Bethlehem-babe-turned-Christ would one day teach, is found within. That breathtaking Christmas hymn, O Holy Night, perhaps says it best:

> *"Long lay the world in sin and error*
> *pinning until He appeared and*
> *the soul felt its' worth"*

A new-born doesn't speak; it has no doctrine to offer; no morality to espouse. The new-born Christ mirrors in us possibility and potential, value and self-worth. Perhaps in our particular time and history of salvation we, like our NONE contemporaries, and like those shepherds of old, need to step back from the rigors of religion and seek the divine in the ordinary.

To seek the kingdom of heaven within, beyond or before doctrine or the dictates of morality, abandoning ourselves to the Advent star or the singing of the angels; to be led to where we need to be ~~ in grateful appreciation for our soul's worth. For as conduits of the divine, starry-eyed and delirious, we know what Einstein posited, that the past and the future are only illusions, that Advent IS Christmas. The waiting is always over ~~ we just haven't realized it yet.

 Father Tom Brosnan

A Crooked Advent Wreath

I have an Advent wreath…it is crooked. Someone asked me why I didn't get a new one. I explained that it was crooked from the day I got it. It was made by my special ed students. One student said, "it's not perfect, but it sure was made with love".

Remember… your light might sometimes feel dim
or just be a small little flicker
but it sure can be full of love.

Advent sheds light on…
>...struggles of the human heart
>...despair of war and violence
>...woundedness of addictions
>...heartaches of sorrow and loss
>...worries of family life
>...darkness of depression

The wonderful holy lights of Advent help us to birth...

> ...love into life
> ...a welcome for the lonely
> ...a comfort for the sorrowful
> ...being a bearer of hope
> ...a trust that can let go
> ...a resting place for
> > the weary

We become with the
Advent~~Christmas season
> lights for the world
> > shining a deep faith-filled radiance
> > of compassion
> > > born of holy humility.

Lord, let me be your Bethlehem light.

Advent Reflections

1. How will you faithfully share faith, hope and charity this Advent season?
2. How will you make room in the inn of your heart this Advent?
3. Where in your life does the light of Christ most seek a welcome?
4. What is yearning in your heart this season?
5. What needs to happen in your life to enable you to be more open and receptive to the yearnings of the world?
6. Think of the people and events in your life that have encouraged you and deepened your hope to be Jesus' love here on earth?

Write and Advent Prayer that begins with

Come Lord Jesus...

Shine Forth...

 Where can you share your sacred light...
...on a quiet stroll in winter time
...visiting a neighbor
...looking into the eyes of the person working in a supermarket stocking shelves and saying have a really good day
...giving coffee respectfully to a homeless person
...praying for all the people (adults and children) killed in senseless shootings ~~ pray for the families
...putting a donation in a box at a store that says "for those in need"
...sharing a light of comfort and peace for a person experiencing sorrow or loss

Where will you shine your light today?

How will you shine your light today?

Who will you shine your light with today?

Who might shine their light for you?

May these Stars of Divine Love and Grace shine through you.

1. Let the <u>Star of Hope</u> blaze through discouragement, doubt or fear.

2. Let the <u>Star of Kindness</u> radiate through what you think, feel and do today.

3. Let the <u>Star of Understanding</u> beam acceptance to those with whom you have any difficulty.

4. Let the <u>Star of Laughter</u> sparkle in your eyes and in your smile.

5. Let the <u>Star of Openness</u> be a wide ray of love for those who are different than you.

6. Let the <u>Star of Courage</u> grow bright in whatever requires your inner strength.

7. Let the <u>Star of Forgiveness</u> draw you nearer to those with whom you feel alienated.

☆

8. Let the <u>Star of Gratitude</u> encourage you to be generous with your gifts.

9. Let the <u>Star of Justice</u> lead you to speak out in order to change an injustice today.

10. Let the <u>Star of Faith</u> beam through you by what you say and do.

11. Let the <u>Star of Charity</u> keep you balanced in tending to the needs of self and others.

12. Let the <u>Star of Compassion</u> draw you into the world's wide expanse of suffering.

13. Let the <u>Star of Love</u> shine through you to all persons especially those with special needs.

14. Let the <u>Star of Peace</u> be a ray of steadfast calmness.

Advent is a sacred and wonderful Pilgrimage of Light

> **Awesome**
>> **Reverent**
>>> **Radical**
>>>> **Suffused**
>>>>> **Inspired**

> **Comforting**
>> **Consoling**
>>> **Glorious**
>>>> **Peaceful**
>>>>> **Prayer-filled**

What five words can you add to describing Advent?

1.

2.

3.

4.

5.

Write a prayer using any three words from above list about your Advent Pilgrimage.

Advent is a "reminder"
a well needed one
to set aside time to pray
for the graces needed
to truly value the
reality of
"Emmanuel-God-with-us"
and all that this
amazing gift means

Sister Peggy McVetty, O.P.

1. How will you set aside some Advent~~Christmas time in a meaningful way?
2. What does "Emmanuel-God-with-us" mean to you, not just during Advent...but every day?
3. Name an "amazing"grace you have received ... and how do you share it?

Innkeeper

 We have a wonderful choice to invite Jesus into our daily life in how we…
…speak respectfully
…engage with compassion
…embrace diversity

Let us make room with our…
…time   …trust
…presence   …acceptance
…better listening   …charity
…comfort   …forgiveness

Making room will not always feel comfortable, in fact it can feel quite uncomfortable and unsettling, very challenging but inspiring…it can give birth to hope.

How can you (me too) be an Innkeeper?

1.
2.
3.
4.
5.

Describe an Innkeeper in one word.   Tell why.

Litany of an Innkeeper

Response: *I open my heart.*

I am the Innkeeper, I love this humble inn, every dusty corner of it...it is my Bethlehem home.

<u>Let us pray quietly</u>

I am the Innkeeper, it is said the Lord is coming, will my inn be ready for him?

<u>Let us pray quietly</u>

I am the Innkeeper, I give pilgrim travelers room in what I have left...a stable, a manger with straw.

<u>Let us pray quietly</u>

I am the Innkeeper, tired and weary, I listen and hear the angels singing over my poor stable.

<u>Let us pray quietly</u>

I am the Innkeeper, I kneel humbly before the manger...knowing in my heart helping others will be helping Jesus born in a stable in my Bethlehem.

Let us pray quietly

I am the Innkeeper, with one last look at the little baby with his mother, I leave the stable to begin to live a new and different life found in a little town called Bethlehem.

Let us pray quietly

We are the Innkeepers...outside the stable the sun shines ever so brightly and deep inside each one of us now knows we are part of the brightness of the holy message...born in a stable.

Let us pray quietly

You are a "Modern" Innkeeper

1. Who do you hear knocking?
2. What do you say to those knocking?
3. How do you make room in your heart?
4. What does it mean to be an innkeeper?
5. What gift do you "become" at the stable?

Write a Prayer called... A Modern Innkeeper

A Parable About...A Little Blind Lamb

 One day shepherds were on their way to Bethlehem to see the newborn king. In the distance they could hear angels singing "Glory to God". A little blind lamb was close by and heard the shepherds talking of a great light that was leading them. The little blind lamb decided to follow them, and as he did, he felt the warmth of the light in his heart.

The little blind lamb wondered what would this new king look like. He wondered because he could not see. The little blind lamb heard the shepherds saying how bright the lights were as the angels sang of peace. He heard the angels and the message they sang was full of love and joy. It made him feel so peace-filled, happy and content.

The journey through the night seemed to be one of a renewed feeling of joy and hope. The little blind lamb felt a sense of trust he had not felt for so long. The evening of following a light (within) gave him new courage and a sense of being loved just as he was.

The shepherds too seemed more quiet and reflective on the night's journey of only having one bright star to follow. They spoke of "looking up" and believing more in the promise of "God with them..."

One shepherd noticed that the little blind lamb had followed them and commented on the "least" being welcomed. The shepherds had found this little lamb lost and alone. They left the 99 to save him. The little blind lamb never forgot their kindness.

 It made the little blind lamb feel so happy when he heard the shepherds say that the newborn king comes for all. Now he too, was on a very special pilgrimage to give a welcome to the newborn king. The little blind lamb shed a tear of joy. The light from the star leading them shone a radiance on his tear as it led the shepherds and the little blind lamb down a hillside to a stable.

There the shepherds knelt in prayer, adoration and wonder. The little blind lamb sensed this awe and wonder. He slowly made his way (feeling the light within) to sit next to the manger. As he did, a great and glorious light shone down and warmed the little blind lamb's heart. As he looked up...for the first time in his life...he SAW! The newborn king is a little baby he thought...a little one amongst us showing us that the least shall be the best gift of all.

The little blind lamb gave a "baaaa" as the angels sang, "peace to all" and "this is my beloved son". The shepherds watched in wonder as they saw that the little lamb was no longer blind but could see. They too felt that they could see in new ways. As one of the shepherds picked up the little lamb, the little baby-Christ touched the little lamb and a light shone so bright that all hearts throughout the world were united in love.

(John 9:25 "...and now I can see....")

The angels sang... "Glory to God" with glorious~~

    ...simplicity   ...faithfulness
    ...humility   ...peace-giving
    ...trust   ...love
    ...hope   ...joy

Glory to God...with the least.

The shepherds on their return journey to the hillside where they tended the sheep were ever so happy to see the little lamb so happy tending to the other sheep with his beautiful heart that shone so deeply of God's love. The little lamb showed them that on this humble hillside is where God's Glory would forever shine.

The little lamb told the other sheep that when the little baby touched him, he saw a print of a heart on his paw. The shepherds saw it too. One shepherd said you will now be called "Little Pax" (Peace). You have been given a special blessing~~ to see with peace.

You were blind...and now you see
We too were blind...and now we see

Little Pax (Peace) looked up to the sky at the Bethlehem Star shining ever so brightly. He now knew that his new sight was a blessing that would forever give Glory to God. With our humble sight...let us too be a blessing of peace.

Pacem in Terris~~Peace on Earth (Encyclical~1963 Pope John XXIII)

The O Antiphons share different titles of the Messiah. They help us to know who Jesus is and help us to deepen our awareness of Christ being reborn in our hearts and spirits every day but especially during the Advent~~Christmas season.

O Highest Wisdom come...
O Lord of Israel come...
O Root of Jesse come...
O Key of David come...
O Glorious Dayspring come...
O King of Nations come...
O God Among Us come...

Now just take one O antiphon and pray it slowly with your pilgrim thoughts.
(Do this for 5 minutes)

Write your prayer here. Begin it with...O

O...

O Highest Wisdom... (Isaiah 11:2-3)
Let us dare to live the wisdom of God's word in our daily lives.

> *The light of God's Wisdom shines in darkness and the darkness shall not overcome it.* (John 1:1-5)

> *O Lord, fill our hearts today.*

What action of holy wisdom can you share today?

O Lord of Israel... (Gal. 6: 1-5)
If we listen carefully and bring our hearts to the spiritual message of Christ being born, we will hear the call to come and companion one another...bear one another's burden(s).

> *O Lord, fill our hearts today.*

What action of compassion can you "be" today?

O Root of Jesse... (Isaiah 11: 1, 10)
The "root" of hope, peace, joy and faith dwell in our hearts...let them take a deeper root in your daily lives especially during this holy Advent~~Christmas season.

O Lord, fill our hearts today.

What action of hope can you share that brings new life to another human being?

O Key of David... (Rev. 3: 7, 1-12)
Who has the Key of David opens a door of the heart and no one is shut out.

The Key is...
- ...hospitality
- ...acceptance
- ...presence
- ...encouragement
- ...welcome
- ...an open heart

O Lord, fill our heart today.

What action will you take today with your key?

O Glorious Dayspring... (Isaiah 9:1-2)

The people who walked in darkness have seen a great light; those who lived in a land of deep darkness~~on them light has shone.

O Lord, fill our hearts today.

What action can you take today that is filled with the tender mercy of God?

O King of Nations... (Ephesians2: 17-22)
The Lord shares restoring graces. The stone that the builder rejected has become the cornerstone... (Matthew 21: 33-42)

O Lord, fill our hearts today.

What action of restorative justice can you share in ordinary humane ways?

O God Among Us... (Isaiah 7:14)

 "...the young woman is with child and shall bear a son and name him Emmanuel~~God is with us."

May the joy of knowing that Christ dwells among us in a variety of holy ways...fill us with the Christmas spirit of becoming God's love for one another.

O Lord, fill our hearts today.

What action can you take today of being Love "incarnate" so someone else feels hope and joy?

O how will you be a Christ-Bearer of the holy lights of Advent-Christmas time?

The "O Antiphons" do not just remind us that the Lord is ever present in the world. They tell us that we each are called to "incarnate" the message and meaning of the O Antiphon into our Advent~~ Christmas pilgrimage and on into the New Year.

The message of "Come" is a holy invitation to be the heart, feet, arms, and spirit of God's love here on earth.

Joanne Kennedy...Catholic Worker~~Mary's House
        in NYC
Sister Flor de Maris Buruca, O.P.~~
        Visitation Community
Sister Ruth Lautt, O.P.~~ St. Fidelis Street Ministry
Father Frank Pizzarelli~~Hope House Ministries
Rev. William Barber~~Poor Peoples' Campaign
Sister Norma Pimentel~~Catholic Charities
        at the Border
Archbishop Gustavo Garcia-Siller~~
        A Shepherd's Voice

Name some people that you know that share the O Antiphons in their ordinary lives in extraordinary ways.

How do you share the O Antiphons in your life?

Advent~~Christmas Thoughts from a Spiritual Heart

Aaaah ... calm and quiet in church. While the outside world gets busier and busier those last two weeks before Christmas, church is filled with images of love ~~ Mary and Joseph.

For me, St. Joseph communicates heart to heart deep feelings...
>...trust
>...loving presence
>...kindness

The Hymn~~Adeste Fidelis is my favorite. Its lyrics sing of being *faithful* and being called by God to behold God's love in our life and to give glory to God ... the Light of Lights.

Father Thomas (Tom) Ahern

St. Joseph...a <u>Light of Trust</u>

St. Joseph reminds us that the pilgrimage of the quiet deep Advent lights that faith holds will bring us to a new Bethlehem.

St. Joseph reminds us that the message of following the Lord will reside deep within our spirit and help us to go forward with a hope rooted in divine love.

St. Joseph reminds us that better listening will encourage us to respond to God's will with great courage and commitment.

St. Joseph reminds us that actions speak more deeply than mere words~~actions that shine with God's love.

I am following Love...How?
I am sharing Love...How?
I am becoming Love...How?
I am Loving...How?

Sit quietly as you meditate on the holy silence where St. Joseph learned to trust with a great light.

Name that light... become that light in your pilgrimage.

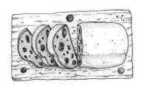

Advent~~Christmas Recipes

Advent~~Christmas Days
at
The Kitchen Table

Hold the warmth of your kitchen brew and reflect on your pilgrimage with some warm light-filled recipes.

Fruit-filled Stollen
Linzer Cookies
Baked Apples in Mulled Wine
Spritz Cookies
German Rum Truffles
Cinnamon Star Cookies
Apple Strudel
Gingerbread House
Anisette Biscotti
Eggnog Bundt Cake
Bambino Bread

Father Dominic Garramone, OSB has a recipe for Bambino bread that is available online. Bambino Bread represents the Christ Child in swaddling clothes. Father Garramone helps us see the scripture meaning in baking during the holiday season.

I have made this Bambino Bread and served it at a morning Advent~~Christmas Brunch Retreat.

An Advent~~Christmas Recipe

Advent is a recipe that is full of wonderful, holy lights of inspiration and transformation.

Prepare your Advent~~Christmas Recipe one day at a time out of these shining ingredients:

Mix well each day...
>1 light of brightness that brings inspiration and assures us of our courage
>1 small light of brightness called generosity that stirs into life how kindness can help everyone live life better

Add to each day of Advent~~Christmas time:
>1 light of a prayer of believing even when you have some doubts
>1 light of sacrifice that brings a sense of peace to someone else

Sprinkle some small lights of justice that sparkle peace-filled thoughts of hope into places of discouragement, war, violence, and discord.

Serve your recipe of lights in a "vessel of love" with one's faith shining so radiantly that little sparkles of transformation begin to rise.

Treasure your recipe.
The best way to treasure it
is to serve it every day
in some life-giving way.

What Advent~~Christmas Recipe will you share during this season?
What is the name of your recipe?
My recipe name is..
"Clothe Yourselves With Love"
(Colossians 3: 12-14)

 What ingredients are in your recipe? Is your recipe "full of light"?

What recipe would you like others to share with you?

In exchanging our recipes…. we become more of the light and the light gets brighter.

Ornament Names

How would you like to decorate a Universal Christmas tree? Perhaps with ornaments of...

...kinder words
...healing wounds
...compassionate attentiveness
...faith-filled trust
...joyful service
...affirming actions
...Christ-Bearing friendship

Choose one of the above or write your own ornament name. Write a Prayer called...
My Holy Ornament.

Advent~~Christmas Words
that Inspire

Hope	Prophecy	Peace
Bethlehem	Stable	Shepherd
Love	Angels	Waiting
Trusting	Prepare	Justice
Mercy	Joy	Manger
Star	Innkeeper	Donkey
Kings	Gifts	Straw
Hillside	Magnificat	Novena

Circle 5 words that you would like to meditate on and then write a prayer using the 5 words.

DECEMBER

There are __ days left to Christmas. You see these signs in ads and on store windows. It can become a stressful time. Here are some prayerful thoughts for all of us to consider on our Advent~~Christmas pilgrimage.

Advent ~~ words that immediately pop into my and maybe your mind are: waiting, preparing, belonging and longing for that deeper relationship with God incarnate. Sitting with God, I come to realize that God has been waiting patiently for me!

As a child all the anxiety that was built up around this time of year. In my house we never saw a present, a tree or train set village till Christmas morn. To this day my siblings and I marvel how our parents managed to do that. Keeping it all a surprise! It was simpler then-counting the days, making my "being good" list and hoping...

As an adult, I, like everyone, are constantly surrounded with all the chaos that is attached to the "holy" season. One must make the effort to be still and allow the incarnation to take hold of me.

This is the Advent I treasure each year. The time, moments that I am still and hear God speaking to me. It is a special time for me to reflect on our Blessed Lady. She is the first model for all, especially for women to grasp the true, simple meaning of holding and being close to her Son. Birthing!

Meister Eckhart, a Dominican theologian, writes so beautifully, *"We are all meant to be mothers of God for God is always needing to be born."* May this holy season be all that and more for all of us. The grace to birth God in our needy world.

Sister Pat Hanvey, O.P.

What is the best "Gift" that we can give or receive during this Advent~~Christmas season?

Name some spiritual gifts...
1.
2.
3.
4.

Hmmmm...
Perhaps the sheep and
donkey and oxen in the
stable remind us of
creation's sharing of the radiant light

the gift of quiet ordinary presence

Perhaps the Advent~~Christmas season can
be one of decorating the world with...
    ...peace-filled words and deeds
    ...a listening heart that does not judge
    ...genuine and sincere kindness

the gift full of tender mercy and
compassion

In the darkness Christ was born and there he
brought the light of peace. So too, our faith
can shine hope in the midst of difficulties,
loss, hurt and deep wounds.

the gift of transformation is a holy light

Name the gift...
  ...you want to share
  ...you would like to receive

Radiant Lights...

    ...help us to celebrate life

    ...help us to share peace

    ...help us to shine with patience

    ...help us to be still and know God
        more

Radiant Lights Shine...

    ...Mary's Yes

    ...Joseph's Trust

    ...Shepherd's Faith

    ...Wisemen's Courage

    ...Angel's Message

    ...Innkeeper's Hospitality

    ...Jesus' Presence

There are people who possess and radiate the goodness of God through their own pilgrimage of sharing the lights.

Sister Mary Hughes, O.P.
Father Bob Lauder
Sister Mary Anna Euring, O.P.
Mother Teresa of Calcutta
Sister Thea Bowman
Arthur Mirell
Sister Irene Weiner, O.P
Lori Mergen
Sister Ellen Glavey, RSM.
Peg Franco
Jo Cardone
Father Tom Ahern
Susan Schwemmer
Sister Lenore Toscano, O.P.
Roseann Maggio
Sister Diane Morgan, O.P.
Julie Pallioto
Sister Marilyn Breen, O.P.
Shant Kizakian
Hildemarie Ladouceur
James Ragusano

Add some names of people that radiate the goodness of the wondrous lights for you.
1.
2.
3.

Dwelling Place

Jesus is present with us on our Advent~~Christmas pilgrimage. He invites us to go deeper into the journey of becoming the lights of love, peace, joy and hope. Let us glow with joy and shine like the sun (son).

 Sing: *This Little Light of Mine* (add a special witness word to each verse)

We all are Bearers of the Light.
We share our light in a variety of ways.

Joy-Giver...Syed Naqvi at Barney's Service Station
Unwavering Trust...Sister Fran Gorman, O.P.
Contagious Faith...Sister Peggy McVetty, O.P.
Friendly Service...Tom Mullane at Bayside Farm
Unconditional Love...Joan Kovacs
Heart Peace Spirits...Adolofo and Judy Quezada
Prayer Companion...Sister Mary John O'Carm.
Loyal Stewardship...Sister Pat Koehler,O.P.
Light of Kindness...Dr. Gloria Durka, Ph.D
Disciple of Compassion...Peg Franco
Caring Light...Barbara Douvas-Kyprianides

A Galaxy of Lights...

How do you adjust the light to
meet the world's unanswered needs?

Sometimes life seems to hide the light in...

...war and discord
...difficulties and problems
...lack of charity and hope
...fears and anxieties
   (personal and global)

Advent~~Christmas time draws us toward the
Divine Light that...
   ...warms a human yearning with renewed
         hope
   ...sees beyond a closed heart
   ...offers healing full of holy compassion
   ...brings heart peace to a broken and
         wounded world

Where is Christ's "radiance" born
   in your life?

How do you share it?

How do you deepen that "radiance" in your life and
for the world community?

One of my friends (James Palmaro) who shares his wonderful poems for my books has been blind since age 27. What I have learned through his poems written from his heart is  that we walk by faith and not by sight.

(2 Corinthians 5-7)

During Advent~~Christmas season this scripture passage comes alive by trusting and believing that God is preparing us for blessings filled with wonderful, life-giving lights here on earth.

The best gift of light that we can share is...
...being kind and attentive to others' needs
...slow down and put more of Christ' love
   into this season
...like St. Joseph, be a person who
   cherishes the light
...like Mother Mary~~ hold peace in your
   heart.

Jo Cardone and Julie Paliotta
(sisters)

"All the darkness in the world cannot extinguish the light of a single candle."
(St. Francis of Assisi)

CHRISTMAS IS FULL OF THE ABUNDANCE OF GOD'S LOVE

The Broken Manger

I saw a broken manger one cold December night
Beside a sidewalk trash bin, beneath a lamppost
      light
No one seemed to notice, they just hurried right
      on by
As colored lights and Christmas sights captured
      every eye
Chimes and songs and rushing throngs filled the
      frosty air
As advertising billboards encouraged us to "share"
There were shopping bags, pricey tags and flashing
      neon signs
Checks and desks of credit cards and crowded
      cashier lines

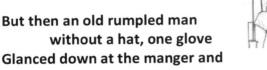

But then an old rumpled man
      without a hat, one glove
Glanced down at the manger and
      his heart was filled with love
It reminded him of childhood, of a Christmas he
      once knew
It reminded him of Jesus, of peace and kindness too

He reached down for the manger and he handled it
      with care
As tears of joy streamed down his face, glistening
      his hair

He mended every sign post with string that he
     had found
While sleeping on some cardboard nearby a school
     playground

He headed toward the corner church and dreamt
     of midnight mass
And upon the barn he placed a star he made from
     shards of glass
With growing pride and pep and passing every store

He reached the highest church step and
     stretched out for the door

But the heavy wooden latch was locked,
     this wasn't Christmas day
A little boy then grasped his hand and
     told him we could pray
Then the man remembered, and his eyes
     grew bright and wide
He squeezed the boy's right hand and said
     "we can enter from the side!"
They blessed the mended manger with
     water in the hall
They slowly walked the center aisle and
     saw Jesus on the wall

They placed the precious gift beneath
     the glowing tree
Then with awe and reverence they bent
     down on one knee

They thanked the Lord for Christmas
and sang a song of joy
He felt the warmth of Christmas and
then he hugged the boy

When I went to bed later that night
I thought of the meaning implied by the sight
Of a manger left abandoned, discarded, ignored
Until a man and a child had its' beauty restored
Revealing a truth so deep and profound
It can only be seen from within looking down

(James Palmaro, a gifted poet, with heart-words written in prose. He himself is disabled with blindness but looks within and sees the world through his faith well-lived.)

Advent~~Christmas Holy Heart-Pilgrims

The Holy Heart-Pilgrims are:
John the Baptist
Elizabeth
Mother Mary
St. Joseph
An Innkeeper
Shepherds
Wise Men

They carry the message of God...a message of peace
and love, hope, and joy.

Very often this message gets diminished by
the commercialism and materialism of life.

We are encouraged during this season to try
to have a balance of material gift giving and
spiritual heart-peace giving.

Meditate on the Holy Heart-Pilgrims and you will
find better ways of being and relating...

> ...from selfishness to selflessness
> ...from arrogance to respect
> ...from harshness to compassion
> ...from gossip to kindness

I am sure there are people in your own life that you believe are truly Holy Heart-Pilgrims.

Maybe, just maybe, they are the people whose faith inspires others and who understand that the pilgrimage of stirring the lights is when you begin to comprehend that there is more to life than what's here on earth.

What Holy Heart-Pilgrim in scripture (or on your earthly pilgrimage) has shone a great light?

Share ... Find someone to share your reflection. Hmmmm... it might even be the person that radiates a beautiful, holy light!

 My special High School friends sure left beautiful lights of holy cherished memories in my heart...

Kathy Tully

Carol Donohue

Marlene Martin

Laura Burke

Jackie D'Antonio

Marilyn Melzer

Sharon Brady

Linda Sue Galate

Mary Ann Jansen

Rosemary Mergen

Joan Volpe

Beverly Ryan

Patricia Waller

Jackie Cocozza

Reflection from a Holy Heart-Pilgrim...

Advent is a season of waiting...a season of preparation, a time of excitement. It's a time of "getting ready" because my Savior is about to be born! I think of the song "Prepare Ye the Way of the Lord". The joy of knowing someone special is about to arrive!

During this holy season I hear the message of patience, I hear the call to stop, look, and listen. To stop the busyness and take a moment to be still and enjoy the simplicity of life; to look up to the heavens and ask myself... do you see your shining, guiding star? To listen to the preparation of waiting. To ask, what are you waiting for? What does my waiting look like? I share God's love by being present. Sometimes no words are needed. Sometimes the only thing I can do is to love someone and wait with them in the midst of their quietness for their delivery.

An Advent message needed in every human heart is to be reminded that every human has one. Every human has a heart and a message of patience. Advent offers the gift of hope and love and joy and peace.

Advent offers the gift of Jesus.

 My favorite Advent light is purple. Why purple? Purple is the color of royalty. A reminder that I am a King's kid, heir to the throne of Love. My Advent prayer is a personal one... "as I prepare and wait for your birth, O Lord, let me walk in hope, love, joy and in your light of peace. Give me the patience not to wander, but to be still and wait in patience." The figure of Advent~~Christmas that inspires me are the Magi, The Three Kings. In their quietness, they traveled to follow a star, trusting that it would lead them to their newborn King...and it did!

Joan Davenport

Reflect on Joan's sharing...

> What is your favorite Advent color...and why?
>
> Why does our world need the gift of patience?
>
> How do you share patience?
>
> Who is your favorite Advent~~Christmas figure and why?

Advent~~Christmas season immerses us in the unfolding of wonderful, sacred lights.

Plants flourish with the light.
Human beings flourish <u>within the light.</u>

What does it mean to flourish?

Where can we find light?
Read Amanda Gorman's poem:
<u>The Hill We Climb</u>

Each week of Advent we take a pilgrimage of carrying a new light that gives us a vision that changes and expands with each new day. As our vision of what Christmas is all about is embraced, we dare to carry within us a renewed faith of the healing lights into the darkness of…

poverty	disrespect
racism	great sorrow
war	toxic anger
rudeness	gun violence
violence	abuse
hatred	terrible gossip

What do we learn, see and feel about how other pilgrims live with the light(s) of their Advent~~Christmas pilgrimage?

These lights dare to be prophetic...
  Sister Joan Chittister O.S.B.
    (Co-Chair of Global Peace
    Initiative of Women)
  Bishop Thomas Gumbleton
    (Social Activist)
  Dorothy Day
    (The Catholic Worker~~Mary's House,
    NYC)
  Father Gustavo Gutierrez, O.P.
    (Preferential Option for the Poor)

 We are all called to be prophetic in how we live and share our faith...and see it in others who proclaim it so courageously.

A Prophetic sharing...

As we journey during this Advent~~Christmas season, we light the prophetic candle of the Advent wreath that represents hope. Through the Scripture readings of the liturgical season, we are reminded of the prophecies that foretold the coming of the Messiah. People of faith had to wait a long time for the actual birth of the Savior, Jesus Christ. A friend of mine, Sister Ramon, used to say that "God-waiters get good tips." It is incredible that prophets actually predicted so many years before how Jesus would be born to a Virgin Mother. Sometimes, we may doubt whether the promises of God's faithfulness and heavenly reward are real or just wishful thinking on our part. Even people of faith may wonder whether God's promises are any different from the fantasy of Santa Claus bringing gifts to good boys and girls. Remembering that the ancient prophecies were fulfilled with the birth of Our Lord gives us hope that God's undying care in this life and the promise of heavenly reward in the next life are for real. Lighting that Candle of Prophecy on the Advent wreath helps to dispel the darkness of our own doubts and open our hearts to the renewed life of Christ being rekindled within us on our earthly pilgrimage.

Sister Alice Byrnes, O.P.

Name three modern day prophets...

1.

2.

3.

Some Dominican Prophets I know...

Sister Elizabeth Gnam, O.P.

Sister Jeanne Clark, O.P.

Sister Sally Butler, O.P.

Sister Margaret Galiardi, O.P.

Sister Vicki Toale, O.P.

Sister Mary Pat Neylon, O.P.

This holy season is a time where we can see
a glimpse of Jesus' light in one another...

...a friend who is ever so honest about
herself

...a friend who has a deeply, faithful
prayer life

...a person whose heart is so generous
in hidden and extraordinary ways

...a person who helps others to bear
their cross with a heart that is full of
compassion

Each light of Advent helps us to take life's pilgrimage very often into an unknown space and believe that there one will discover more of the light to become and to bear for another.

So much news about...

>...war
>...violence
>...hate

Yet in the ember of a small ash of wanting peace is the light for a new day, a new beginning...a light that calls for peace and calm.

Silent Night, Holy Night
>All is calm, all is bright!

The "calm" is knowing God is with us... Emmanuel. God is with us in our fears, sorrows and even in our own personal, daily annoyances, failures and missteps. All is bright in the presence of the radiant light that helps to show us that creating a more just world order will come when each and every one's light is a bearer of mercy, compassion, forgiveness and healing.

Light filters through discord, disregard, ignorance and discomfort. It has a center that is deep and energizes our very human pilgrimage with an everlasting grace-filled light.

These lights are...
...Good News
...Holy Scripture
...Transforming Messages
...Inspiring Witnesses
...Challenging Actions
...Heart-Peace Connections

Add your message of these lights...
1.
2.
3.
4.

The Sankofa Muse

"Until None Need Stars To Call Them On"
"they were overjoyed at seeing the stars…"
(Matthew 2:1-12)

Moving west for days that blended into a forever
                                    now
our minds locked into each other's vision
                                    and the star
defied all the knowledge we had hungrily held
each night it called us
the calm and steady trust brought to us
by that flickering light
                                    was nearly drowned
by the pinched face and the slicing words
of this hungry king whose fear
assaulted us
            from the moment
we gave him our cause

That night we did not share a word
of what we felt
        we slept
                we allowed our dreams
to wrap us in a cloud
And when we found the child   we gave them
of our treasures

and our hoarded dreams
and whispered
Leave
    so that what our hearts can barely contain
when following this child's eyes
                will survive
until done need stars
to call them on

Poem by Rev. Joseph A. Brown, S.J.
Professor of Africana Studies
Southern Illinois University
at Carbondale.
Father Joseph Brown, S.J. is the author of
"The Sankofa Muse"
http://sankofamuse.blogspot.com/

Reread the poem slowly a few times.
Sit quietly in prayer.

What beautiful light do you discover in
reading and praying the poem?

Thoughts on the flickering light....

Christmas...

> is a time to open our hearts to the wondrous lights of holiness that invites us to rediscover more of Jesus love right <u>in our midst.</u>

Christ is our light.

Christ reminds us that we are always "becoming"...

...more hopeful
...more faithful
...more joy-filled
...more peaceful
...more loving

The world is not as just, not as loving, not as kind as we know it can and should and could be. The coming of Christ and His presence among us, as one of us, gives us reason to live with hope that the wonderful light of holiness will shatter the darkness so that we can each be liberated from our fears and believe that we are never alone or abandoned.

Christmas is a holy time to be "transformed" as we dare to become more reflective of the light of God's love in our ordinary and daily life encounters especially those that challenge us and call us forth to rebirth justice for all.

Christmas is a Holy Pilgrimage...

Oh yes, there will be presents, parties and tree trimmings and advent wreaths hung...and candles lit. All of this is wonderful but let us be reminded that the spiritual meaning of this season is to bring Jesus' love to earth.

Christ is born in us today
in order that he may appear
to the whole world through us.
(Thomas Merton)

How is Christ being reborn in you during this holy season?
1.
2.
3.

Listen with holy wonder to the message of the hymns:

Silent Night, Holy Night
O Little Town of Bethlehem
O Holy Night
Away In A Manger
Joy to the World
We Three Kings

As you listen to the message of these holy hymns you will be reminded of how Mary and Joseph, the shepherds and the Three Kings became the holy listeners of God's message of love being born in human hearts. In the holy prayer-filled silence of this Christmas season you and I can choose to center our hearts with God's ways. Be a holy listener as you hum along with your favorite Christmas hymn and feel the holy light dwelling within your spirit.

Listen to my Special Ed Students

Do you believe in Santa Claus?
You should!
It is Jesus dressed in a red suit.

I have six cents.
Keep it as a gift.
It will make you smile!

I don't want God to leave my heart.
I told him I would share ½ my favorite
    sandwich with him.

Do we hear and see the God of Love in
unassuming people, places and events?

Who has surprised you with God's Love?
(that ½ sandwich ended up on my desk!)

What gifts can we share that don't need
    any wrapping?

Hmmmm...

...being sincere

...sharing kindness

...forgiving with mercy

...being generous with affirmations

...respecting each other's vulnerability

...extending charity with respect

...always speaking with hope

Write a Prayer about "holy" listening....

During Christmas we see beautifully decorated Christmas trees.

What ornaments can we decorate the Tree of life with?
We decorate by the way we live, serve and share the lights of our Advent~~Christmas pilgrimage.

When you decorate the world with your goodness, charity, peace, patience, trusting and forgiveness you become the "Joy" of the season.   This "Joy" is contagious. It is contagious because of the prayerful spirit behind the gifts, decorated trees and cards.

How would you describe Joy?

Why do you think Joy is contagious?

I know some people who are so joyful that they set the world on fire with God's Joy.

Joe Clark
Sister Laura Helbig, O.P.
Sister Shamus Eileen Dwyer, O.P.
Father Mike Tedone
Sister Judy Flanagan, O.P.
Maryann Gunther
Sister Diane Capuano, O.P.
Sister Kay McCarthy, O.P.
Joanne and John Fanelli

Name some Joy-filled people you know...
1.
2.
3.
4.

Let's give away the spirit of Christmas unwrapped by sharing heart to heart in ordinary ways.

How will you give Joy away?

Who will give it to you?

Give us O Lord, the vision of light that helps us to see your love in this world despite human failures, struggles, lack of patience and inhumane disconnections.

Give us the faith of light, O Lord, to trust in your goodness despite our own personal ignorance, weakness and self-serving ways.

Give us the wisdom that we may continue to be shining lights right where we are knowing that God can do the impossible as He helps us to do what is possible.

Gospel Tree of Life

 **How can our humble light shine more deeply into a world where differences need not divide us, but rather gift us with more loving heart.**

Here are a few suggestions...
...extend peace to one another
...share a kind word
...give sincere comfort to those who feel neglected
...share consolation with those who are bereaved
...give genuine respect to persons struggling
...be a witness of faith-lived well
...have a prayerful heart
...listen with an open heart
...accept one another with charity

Christmas is a holy time...

...to believe Christ is reborn in you
...to recognize the important gifts that
      we share at Christmas are when we
      share ourselves in life-giving ways and
      by doing so we re-shape the world
      with the manger gift of compassionate
      love.
...that in our poorness of spirit, Christ's
      Love shines in our trust, hope and
      peace.
...to believe more in the meaning of "be not
      afraid" that the Child of Bethlehem is
      here to show us the way
...to believe in the silent prayer of
      God with us~~
...that like the Three Kings, we can leave
      Christmas day in another way~~a
      better way

Christmas calls us to draw closer to the
spiritual meaning of Christ living "among us"
so that we too might~~
      Rise up in splendor.

Advent~~Christmas Light of Angels

 Angels have been thought of by St. Thomas Aquinas, O.P. who describes them as creatures of light. These heavenly spirits created by God act as messengers to us on earth whenever God needs us to know, to do, what is good for us as God did when the Angel Gabriel was sent to Mary to ask her to be the Mother of God.

Throughout this holy season the "Spirit of Light" is with us as a reminder. Just as the light of a candle can sometimes appear dimmer than other times, perhaps like us there are those times when we feel the desire for more light as in knowing what to say or to do as we encounter troublesome times in our life. The Advent candles of light during those four weeks are reminders that we always have the brightest light of God within us assuring us that we are never in darkness but have the light of life.

During Advent we surround our spaces at home and in church with the Advent candles, and each week we await the celebration of the memory of Jesus' coming among us. So, in John 8:12 we read, "I am the light of the world, whoever follows me will never walk in darkness but will have the light of life." Gloria … Gloria all the angels sing announcing this wondrous Good News. The light of the angels shine God's love here on earth…and forever and ever.

Sister Laura Helbig, O.P.

Listening Angel Light....
Gabriel listened to Mary

The Angel light is...
> **...attentive**
> **...compassionate**
> **...kindly**
> **...patient**
> **...deeply understanding**
> **...quiet and humble of heart**
> **...prayerful**
> **...nonjudgmental**
> **...serene**
> **...joyful**
> **...loving**

We too during this holy season can practice being...
> **...a good listener**
> **...empathetic**
> **...courageous**
> **...hope-filled**
> **...loving**

Earthen Angels

...ordinary people who carry the light of love
...help others unconditionally
...care for the soil of the earth
...see the connectedness of life as a blessing
...let their lights shine and illuminate even in
   the darkest of places
...encourage everyone with kind words
...show us how God resides within
...pray with us through sorrows and
   hardships

Some "Earthen Angels" I know...
    Mary Morris
    Kathy Accardi
    Sister Barbara Kradick, O.P.
    Kathy Sheridan
    Sister Joan Hartnett, O.P.
    Sister Ginny Connors, O.P.
    Sister Joan Losson, O.P.
    Sister Angela Gannon, C.S.J.
    Sister Anne Sheehan, O.P.

Name some "Angel Lights"
in your life and why.

Light is the garment of an Angel's Message

The Angel Light of Advent~~Christmas leads us to the true meaning of being a light that no darkness can extinguish. Very often the light of an Angel's message is a light that brings peace and comfort to a human spirit.

are they the ones that
wipe away our tears

are they the ones that
comfort our heart losses

are they the ones
that grieve with us

are they the ones
that shoulder the cross with us

are they the ones who
walk through the valley of darkness

perhaps these angel lights show us how
to be comfort and share sympathy and
compassion.

these angels offer us a light
that eases loss, hurts and suffering

these angels invite us to be
a light born of humility in the world

and the angels sang
let there be peace on earth~~

and let it begin...with each one of us.

and we are put on earth a little space
that we may learn to bear the beams of
love for one another.

 the light on an angel wing
touches the heart of God
and is never, ever the same.

How can you bear the beam of love this
Advent~~Christmas season and bring the
angel light of comfort to earth?

Where is the Bethlehem Star Shining?

Light a candle.
Why should we wait in the
darkness?
We light a candle
We want to see
A little...a lot
    a whole lot
Who do you and I want to see?
I ponder this in my heart
Well, who has done the most for me?
Who has had my back (my best interests)
    my whole life?
Who gave His life for me?
I think I'd like to see the Lord~~
Not just me but the family (Clark) is
    all there and
Jesus arrives with two guests
Why Jesus...well, we all owe Him a lot.
I'll listen to anything He says..
(for you I've wanted to travel back
    2000 years or so and be with the disciples
    and hear Jesus speak)
        loaves and fishes
        sermon on the mount
        raising Lazarus

I suspect I could listen to him
a long, long time

Oh, His two guests...
Mary Magdalene because she was always there (apostle of the apostles) so faithful a light.

The other guest ...
would be my old Vietnam friend (I served as a doctor in Vietnam during the war). Her name was Sister San Quentin...a friendly nun who took care of lepers and showed me how these suffering people were fellow human beings. She told me I would remember her name forever. I never forgot her brightness in the midst of war.

I found Bethlehem in an unassuming place where people, me included, were reborn. Bethlehem amidst the darkness in life has a deep light of love that forever shines... right where we are.

Dr. Paul M. Clark, M.D is my older brother whose faith grew brightly because of discovering the Bethlehem light within his own life. He now shares his light tutoring first graders.

Bethlehem Star Shining

You are the light of the Bethlehem Star shining during this holy season and on into the New Year.

Where do you shine?

What is your "Bethlehem" blessing telling the world?

Write your Bethlehem Prayer...

Simplicity of the Spirit of "Giving"

If you consider the dignity of the giver, no gift or no gesture will seem too little to value. No gift is without a blessing.

One day during the Advent-Christmas time in my special ed classroom, I found a gift left on my desk. It was an apple with a bite taken out of it! My special student told me she took a bite out of the apple to make sure that it tasted really good. I thanked my student for the delicious apple.

Every human being is a gift of love, a blessing very often hidden in the humble, holy, ordinary and sometimes extraordinary ways that surprise us with God-lights.

What gift can you share that can become a blessing for someone else?

Advent~~Christmas time is not just a liturgical season but rather a time to be …

> …a reminder of love
> …a blessing
> …a pilgrimage with the holy
> …a renewal of our interior life
> …a redeeming time

"love does not stay idle…"
St. Catherine of Siena

Advent~~Christmas is a "radiant" time to rekindle the lights of…

compassion	charity	kindness
peace	respect	good-will
hope	faith	joy

The gift of the Bethlehem pilgrimage is one that leads to…

> …deep listening
> …gracious compassion
> …wonderful caring

How do you "gift" life
according to God's way?

God's ways are...

ordinary	unexpected
holy	special
extraordinary	challenging
glorious	inspiring
joy-filled	quiet

very often...hidden

and re-discovered with the lights of each new Advent stirring within one human soul on the breath of a God-Advent moment bringing each one of us to Christmas day and on into the light of a New Year.

May each one of us kneel in Bethlehem's light and dare to ignite this holy light into our living and being by becoming the very breath of God's love by embracing all of life's births, deaths and resurrections.

**Jesus is God with us.
Our love is God within us.**

How is God's Love dwelling within you?

Dona Nobis Pacem Song~~

all through the night
seeking the One so long awaited
I followed the light
    now runs a river of love
    and of peace
    born with this child

 Peace...
The message of the season is
so deeply needed in our world
in every human heart

The peace of the Lord's birth is
  one of reconciling love
    and redeeming grace

This is the love that you and I are given
  during the Christmas season.

How will I share God-Peace?

Where does the light of Christ-Peace
most seek a welcome?

Love abounds in all things,
excels from the depths to
beyond the stars,
is lovingly disposed
to all things
(Hildegard von Bingen)

Read my book entitled:

"Be Inspired …To Love"

Take some time reflecting on thoughts and quotes from various people from all walks of life…as well as a few saints who are no longer with us. In doing so, I truly believe you will discover within yourself a "small light" that illuminates God's light out into the Universe. We can do this heart to heart by inspiring one another…*to love*.

Remember...
   a single light dwells within
      truly a beautiful, transforming light
      a holy light
   this light shares the necessary graces
     for each one of us to become
       heart-peace right where we are

The choice to shine is ours as we each...
...climb mountains
...go into valleys
...out into deserts
...and meet detours

  The God of Heart-Peace
    never leaves us

  I am here
  God is here
    leading us onto paths of peace-giving.

<u>On That Holy Mountain</u>~~ (song)

there shall be peace
   led by all the children

     healing on that holy mountain
      justice shall flow'r for all time

and the calf and the lion shall lie down
      on that holy mountain

there shall be peace
holy and peaceful, on that holy mountain

How do you believe that Peace is possible?

What light of Peace leads you?

How do you share the healing balm of
the light of Peace?

Let us like a shepherd of Peace ...
...care for one another
...tend to differences with respect
...let go of indifference
...embrace life with a heart of love

Prophets of Peace…

…proclaim justice for all

…share courageous hope in restorative ways

…live the Gospel call of discipleship

Shepherds of Peace…

…guide others to new life

…protect human rights

…care for the lost among us

Angels of Peace…

…share the message of peace

…become witnesses of peace

…extend loving peace to the marginalized
          in society with dignity

When we are born in the Bethlehem of God's love, we can dare to see the love of Christ shining through the unassuming people and events in life. Can we each let go of being too comfortable and find in the simplicity of the stable the true meaning and blessing of being humble of spirit?

Love born in a stable
is love born in your heart

Christmas...

The Splendor of Star-Light

The holy pilgrimage of the Advent Lights brought our hearts to the manger of the Christ-Child reaching out to bless our faith journey. The glory of daybreak comes as we become Jesus' love reborn again and again.

For Christmas...

I give you a brilliant star

 humble in origin, mighty
with love forever shining
a light in the darkness, a
radiant message of hope
hold it with your heart prayers and you
will become Bethlehem's Love.

It is not far to Bethlehem...
...go to the post office
...go to Barney's Gas Station
...go to Bayside Farm Deli Counter
...go to NorthShore Animal Hospital
...go to your next-door neighbor
...go visit your family/friend
...go stop in at a church or chapel
...go to the silence of your heart

Where is your Bethlehem?

And after Christmas...
...the unwrapping of gifts
...the sharing of memories
...the candles of the wreath all lit and
...the extra candle in the center is lit
   reminding us all that the best gift to share
   is Faith lived, celebrated and shared.

The work (meaning) of Christmas begins
when you and I become the gifts of Jesus
love right where we are...
...caring for those who feel lost
...helping to heal the wounded of spirit
...feeding the hungers of the world
...releasing those who feel oppressed
   unjustly
...rebuilding with humane actions
...radiating the message by our words and
   deeds

 This is when the Glory of God
shines ever so brightly.

Let your "radiant" light of Christmas love shine and may it ignite countless times the message of Jesus being reborn again and again. May this light of Bethlehem shine on into the New Year.

Just what is a "radiant" light?

How do you become a "radiant" light?

Who has been a "radiant" light for you?

How are you a "radiant" light?

1.

2.

3.

The "Love" of Christmas is a love that...
 ...heals
 ...gets into the messiness of life
 ...is costly but necessary
 ...is full of mercy
 ...is inspiring with divine goodness
 ...is uncomfortable forgiveness
 ...recognizes the face of God in the
  hidden and humble
 ...never stops giving forgiveness

Think about this "Love" in Christmas. It is a love that transforms our fears, sorrows and selfishness into lights that create wondrous peace everywhere with everyone.

Our hearts are God's new Bethlehem
where Christ is born anew
It isn't far to Bethlehem
when Christ is born in you

The center of the Pilgrimage of Light begins right in your own human heart that yearns for...

> ...solace   ...acceptance
> ...peace   ...consolation

> give me life renewed
> in the manger and straw
>   of today's faith restored
>   and welcomed

Just pray quietly....

Christmas Gifts....

Every good gift and
every perfect gift
is from above,
and comes down from
the Father of lights.

(James 1:17)

O wondrous gifts when...

...the Divine Companion is always near

...hope reminds us not to lose heart

...life is full of mystery that keeps unfolding

...justice is so bright that it extends out into
the Universe

...the season provides holy moments of
cherishing loved ones

...the Good Shepherd gives us examples of
compassion

...our hearts are united in the simplicity and
humility of a pilgrimage that shares lights
that will forever shine and change each
one of us for the better

A New Year Gift~~
Just might be...
...not a resolution
...nor a promise
that fades

A New Year Gift~~
Just might be...
...a grace of becoming Christ-like in our
daily actions
...a good way of celebrating diversity
...a genuine and sincere way of
restoring peace

A New Year Gift~~
Just might be found...
...in the humility and simplicity of a baby
in a manger reaching out with love to
everyone
...in our hearts kneeling at a manger
filled with hay

**What a gift when
we can say to someone ~~
*"You are a real
gift from God..."***

Epilogue

As we all know, the the Liturgical Advent-Christmas season arrives during the winter. However, I decided to write this book during the summer after thinking that Jesus comes in every season, every day, and to everyone.

Jesus comes to every human heart calling us forth to deepen our faith life and to courageously carry the light and the message of the Advent-Christmas season into our everyday life.

Advent time though four short weeks amidst the flurry of holiday shopping, tree trimming, and gift wrapping is a time of a sacred pilgrimage. It is a holy, quality time to find more love, peace, hope and faith that renews our spirits and shines brightly the real meaning of Christmas when you and I dare to create a sacred time that puts Christ first in our life.

Come, Lord Jesus into...
>...my heart
>...my spirit
>...my soul
>...my longings for peace

Come, Lord Jesus into...
>...my humble words of prayer
>...my acts of hidden charity
>...my gracious forgiveness
>...my compassion for the most
>vulnerable

Come, Lord Jesus into...
>...my discipleship of justice
>...my prophetic life of mercy
>...my efforts to be a source of harmony
>...my sense of solidarity with those who
>are suffering

Come, Lord Jesus into...
>...my sorrows
>...my human longing for respect
>...my failures that teach me patience
>...my limitations that show me better
>ways to trust

Come, Lord Jesus
Come and renew my spirit
Help me to be transformed
Let me shine like the Bethlehem Star~~ a
hope that shares a sparkle of joyous peace
that sows deep and wondrous loving peace
for all of humanity.

What light will you follow into the New
    Year?
What light will you become?
How will you let others share their light?
Who will be the modern innkeeper holding
    the light?

Hopefully, during this winter Advent-Christmas season and on into the New Year of ordinary and sometimes extraordinary time, we will carry the lights and become more of the holy message of the newborn Savior.   Let there be peace on earth and let it begin with each one of us.

...and Jesus was born~~
and we all become
love incarnate

ACKNOWLEDGEMENTS

I would like to thank all the Pilgrim Friends who shared their holy thoughts about Advent-Christmas time and the lights that help us to celebrate Christ's love in our lives.

I especially thank Sister Martin Marie Doran, O.P. for her beautiful, faith-filled message for this book's Prologue. Also note on the Dedication page that Sister Martin is one of this book's "dedicated to" people.

Thank you to my Heart-to-Heart friend and volunteer, Susan Schwemmer, who lights up the world by her selfless gifting of her time and talents especially in helping to get this book as well as my other books published.

Many thanks to Ralph Iskaros who helps to create new holy book cards and flyers along with his extra caring Ministry suggestions. Thank you to my Ink-It Printing Friends of 30 years for creating holy cards and flyers for Heart-to-Heart Ministry with such good quality service. I thank Father Joseph Brown, S.J. who gave permission to share his holy poem in the book.

And once again I extend gratitude to my friend, James Palmaro, who shared two new Poems for this book born out of his love for Christ so well lived with a radiant light of faithfulness.

To all of you who will read this book during the Advent~~Christmas season...I hope you will open this book up anytime in the New Year and renew your commitment to take the holy Pilgrimage of Light everyday of your life and find Jesus reborn in your heart again and again...and again.

Blessings for a Holy and Happy New Year

About the Author

Sister Ave Clark, O.P. is an Amityville, New York Dominican Sister who coordinates Heart to Heart Ministry. Sister is a retreat presenter and a certified, pastoral counselor.

Sister Ave believes that we are all Pilgrim Lights carrying the message of the Advent-Christmas season into a holy New Year by the way in which we each live and share our faith life every day.

Sister Ave prays that the Lord blesses each one of us with the presence of the radiant message of the Bethlehem Star every day in all of our lives where Christ is reborn and celebrated because of our bright, holy and faith-filled light so generously and gracefully shared with one another.

May Advent...the Coming of Christ be shared with...

...everlasting peace
...unconditional love
...radiant hope
...steadfast faithfulness

P.S. ... Remember...

Advent~~Christmas Lights lead us to an extraordinary pilgrimage of sharing Jesus' love.

*Christmas...is love
born in your heart
everyday.*

Other Books by Sister Ave Clark, O.P.

Books are available on Amazon and by
contacting Sister Ave Clark, O.P.
Pearlbud7@aol.com   718-428-2471
www.h2h.nyc

Christmas is most truly
Christmas when we celebrate it
by giving the light of love to
those who need it most....

ADVENT~~CHRISTMAS

A Pilgrimage of Light

*"It's not how much we give;
but how much love
we put into into giving."*

Mother Teresa of Calcutta

A thought to share...

**May our hearts keep vigil each day
this New Year...
as we give birth to Jesus' love**

Light of Christ be with me on my holy pilgrimage

Pray and meditate on your holy pilgrimage today

Merry Christmas

40213239R10097